Ho...

by Iain Gray

Lang Syne
PUBLISHING
WRITING *to* REMEMBER

Lang**Syne**

PUBLISHING

WRITING *to* REMEMBER

79 Main Street, Newtongrange,
Midlothian EH22 4NA
Tel: 0131 344 0414   Fax: 0845 075 6085
E-mail: info@lang-syne.co.uk
www.langsyneshop.co.uk

Design by Dorothy Meikle
Printed by Printwell Ltd
© Lang Syne Publishers Ltd 2017

ISBN 978-1-85217-661-7

Hopkins

MOTTO:
Among the first.

CREST:
A castle in flames.

NAME variations include:
Hopkin
Hopkines
Hopkinson
Hopkyns

Chapter one:

Origins of Welsh surnames

by Iain Gray

If you don't know where you came from, you won't know where you're going is a frequently quoted observation and one that has a particular resonance today when there has been a marked upsurge in interest in genealogy, with increasing numbers of people curious to trace their family roots.

Main sources for genealogical research include census returns and official records of births, marriages and deaths – and the key to unlocking the detail they contain is obviously a family surname, one that has been 'inherited' and passed from generation to generation.

No matter our station in life, we all have a surname – but it was not until about the middle of the fourteenth century that the practice of being identified by a particular, or 'fixed', surname became commonly established throughout the British Isles.

Previous to this, it was normal for a person to be identified through the use of only a forename.

Wales, however, known in the Welsh language as *Cymru*, is uniquely different – with the use of what are known as patronymic names continuing well into the fifteenth century and, in remote rural areas, up until the early nineteenth century.

Patronymic names are ones where a son takes his father's forename, or Christian name, as his surname.

Examples of patronymic names throughout the British Isles include 'Johnson', indicating 'son of John', while specifically in Scotland 'son of' was denoted by the prefix Mc or Mac – with 'MacDonald', for example, meaning 'son of Donald.'

Early Welsh law, known as *Cyfraith Hywel*, *The Law of Hywel*, introduced by Hywel the Good, who ruled from Prestatyn to Pembroke between 915 AD and 950 AD, stipulated that a person's name should indicate their ancestry – the name in effect being a type of 'family tree.'

This required the prefixes *ap* or *ab* – derived from *mab*, meaning 'son of' being placed before the person's baptismal name.

In the case of females, the suffixes *verch* or *ferch*, sometimes shortened to *vch* or *vz* would be attached to their Christian name to indicate 'daughter of.'

In some cases, rather than being known for

example as *Llewellyn ap Thomas* – *Llewellyn son of Thomas* – Llewellyn's name would incorporate an 'ancestral tree' going back much earlier than his father.

One source gives the example of *Llewellyn ap Thomas ap Dafydd ap Evan ap Owen ap John* – meaning *Llewellyn son of Thomas son of Dafydd son of Evan son of Owen son of John*.

This leads to great confusion, to say the least, when trying to trace a person's ancestry back to a particular family – with many people having the forenames, for example, of Llewellyn, Thomas, Owen or John.

The first Act of Union between Wales and England that took place in 1536 during the reign of Henry VIII required that all Welsh names be registered in an Anglicised form – with *Hywel*, for example, becoming Howell, or Powell, and *Gruffydd* becoming Griffiths.

An early historical example of this concerns William ap John Thomas, standard bearer to Henry VIII, who became William Jones.

In many cases – as in Davies and Williams – an s was simply added to the original patronymic name, while in other cases the prefix *ap* or *ab* was contracted to *p* or *b* to prefix the name – as in *ab Evan* to form Bevan and *ap Richard* to form Pritchard.

Other original Welsh surnames – such as Morgan, originally *Morcant* – derive from ancient Celtic sources, while others stem from a person's physical characteristics – as in *Gwyn* or *Wynne* a nickname for someone with fair hair, *Gough* or *Gooch* denoting someone with red hair or a ruddy complexion, *Gethin* indicating swarthy or ugly and *Lloyd* someone with brown or grey hair.

With many popular surnames found today in Wales being based on popular Christian names such as John, this means that what is known as the 'stock' or 'pool' of names is comparatively small compared to that of common surnames found in England, Scotland and Ireland.

This explains why, in a typical Welsh village or town with many bearers of a particular name not necessarily being related, they were differentiated by being known, for example, as 'Jones the butcher', 'Jones the teacher' and 'Jones the grocer.'

Another common practice, dating from about the nineteenth century, was to differentiate among families of the same name by prefixing it with the mother's surname or hyphenating the name.

The history of the origins and development of Welsh surnames is inextricably bound up with the nation's frequently turbulent history and its rich culture.

Speaking a Celtic language known as Brythonic, which would gradually evolve into Welsh, the natives were subjected to Roman invasion in 48 AD, and in the following centuries to invasion by the Anglo-Saxons, Vikings and Normans.

Under England's ruthless and ambitious Edward I, the nation was fortified with castles between 1276 and 1295 to keep the 'rebellious' natives in check – but this did not prevent a series of bloody uprisings against English rule that included, most notably, Owain Glyndŵr's rebellion in 1400.

Politically united with England through the first Act of Union in 1536, becoming part of the Kingdom of Great Britain in 1707 and part of the United Kingdom in 1801, it was in 1999 that *Cynulliad Cenedlaethol Cymru*, the National Assembly for Wales, was officially opened by the Queen.

Welsh language and literature has flourished throughout the nation's long history.

In what is known as the Heroic Age, early Welsh poets include the late sixth century Taliesin and Aneirin, author of *Y Gododdin*.

Discovered in a thirteenth century manuscript but thought to date from anywhere between the seventh and eleventh centuries, it refers to the kingdom of Gododdin that took in south-east Scotland and

Northumberland and was part of what was once the Welsh territory known as *Hen Ogledd*, *The Old North*.

Commemorating Gododdin warriors who were killed in battle against the Angles of Bernicia and Deira at Catraith in about 600 AD, the manuscript – known as *Llyfr Aneirin*, *Book of Aneirin* – is now in the precious care of Cardiff City Library.

Other important early works by Welsh poets include the fourteenth century *Red Book of Hergest*, now held in the Bodleian Library, Oxford, and the *White Book of Rhydderch*, kept in the National Library of Wales, Aberystwyth.

William Morgan's translation of the Bible into Welsh in 1588 is hailed as having played an important role in the advancement of the Welsh language, while in 1885 Dan Isaac Davies founded the first Welsh language society.

It was in 1856 that Evan James and his son James James composed the rousing Welsh national anthem *Hen Wlad Fynhadad – Land of My Fathers*, while in the twentieth century the poet Dylan Thomas gained international fame and acclaim with poems such as *Under Milk Wood*.

The nation's proud cultural heritage is also celebrated through *Eisteddfod Genedlaethol Cymru*, the National Eisteddfod of Wales, the annual festival of music, literature and performance that is held across the nation and which traces its roots back to 1176 when Rhys ap Gruffyd, who ruled the territory of Deheubarth from 1155 to 1197, hosted a magnificent festival of poetry and song at his court in Cardigan.

The 2011 census for Wales unfortunately shows that the number of people able to speak the language has declined from 20.8% of the population of just under 3.1 million in 2001 to 19% – but overall the nation's proud culture, reflected in its surnames, still flourishes.

Many Welsh families proudly boast the heraldic device known as a Coat of Arms, as featured on our front cover.

The central motif of the Coat of Arms would originally have been what was borne on the shield of a warrior to distinguish himself from others on the battlefield.

Not featured on the Coat of Arms, but highlighted on page three, is the family motto and related crest – with the latter frequently different from the central motif.

Echoes of a far distant past can still be found in our surnames and they can be borne with pride in commemoration of our forebears.

Chapter two:

Invasion and conquest

A name of truly martial roots, 'Hopkins' ultimately derives from the Germanic forename 'Hrod-berht', meaning 'famed warrior' or 'renowned fame.'

In common with many others found today – ones that as patronymic surnames derive from a forename and indicate 'son of' – it was by about the eighth century that 'Hrod-berht', meaning 'son of Hob', was adopted by the French to become 'Robert.'

The 'Robert' forename then gave rise to the surnames 'Robert', 'Roberts' and 'Robertson.'

It was in Wales that the form of 'Hob', rather than 'Robert', persisted – explaining why it is here that the surname in the form of 'Hopkins' is particularly identified.

In the now redundant form of 'ab Popkyn', meaning 'son of Popkyn' or 'son of Hopkin', a Johannis ab Popkyn is recorded in the southeast Welsh area of present day Monmouthshire in 1610.

Today the name is particularly prevalent in South Wales which, in common with the rest of the country, was subjected to frequent invasion and conquest.

From about the early fifth century invaders

arrived and settled in the British Isles in the form of the Anglo-Saxons – composed of the Jutes, from the area of the Jutland Peninsula in modern Denmark, the Saxons from Lower Saxony, in modern Germany and the Angles from the Angeln area of Germany.

Further invasion followed between approximately 950 AD and 1000 by the Vikings, and the coastline of Wales was repeatedly subjected to their raids.

When not raping and pillaging, they established trading posts and settlements at modern day Haverfordwest, Fishguard and Caldey Island.

But what was to eventually prove to be the death knell of Welsh independence was sounded in the wake of the Norman Conquest of England in 1066.

A key date in not only English but also Welsh history, by this time England had become a nation with several powerful competitors to the throne.

In what were extremely complex family, political and military machinations, the monarch was Harold II, who had succeeded to the throne following the death of Edward the Confessor.

But his right to the kingship was contested by two powerful competitors – his brother-in-law King Harold Hardrada of Norway, in alliance with Tostig, Harold II's brother, and Duke William II of Normandy.

On October 14, Harold II encountered a mighty invasion force led by William that had landed at Hastings, in East Sussex.

Harold drew up a strong defensive position at the top of Senlac Hill, building a shield wall to repel William's cavalry and infantry.

The Normans suffered heavy losses, but through a combination of the deadly skill of their archers and the ferocious determination of their cavalry they eventually won the day.

Anglo-Saxon morale had collapsed on the battlefield as word spread through the ranks that Harold, the last of the Anglo-Saxon kings, had been killed.

William was declared King of England on December 25, and the complete subjugation of his Anglo-Saxon subjects followed, with those Normans who had fought on his behalf rewarded with lands – a pattern that would be repeated in Wales.

Invading across the Welsh Marches, the borderland between England and Wales, the Normans gradually consolidated gains by building castles, for example in what they called 'Penfro' – later to lend its name to the town of Pembroke.

Under a succession of Welsh leaders who included Llywelyn ap Gruffudd, known as Llywelyn the Last, resistance proved strong.

But it was brutally crushed in 1283 under England's ruthless and ambitious Edward I, who ordered the building or repair of at least 17 castles and in 1302 proclaiming his son and heir, the future Edward II, as Prince of Wales, a title known in Welsh as *Tywysog Cymru*.

Another heroic Welsh figure arose from 1400 to 1415 in the form of Owain Glyndŵr – the last native Welshman to be recognised by his supporters as *Tywysog Cymru*.

In what is known as The Welsh Revolt he achieved an early series of stunning victories against Henry IV and his successor Henry V – until mysteriously disappearing from the historical record after mounting an ambush in Brecon.

Some sources assert that he was either killed in the ambush or died a short time afterwards from wounds he received – but there is a persistent tradition that he survived and lived thereafter in anonymity, protected by loyal followers.

During the revolt, he had consistently refused offers of a Royal Pardon and – despite offers of hefty rewards for his capture – he was never betrayed.

Bearers of the Hopkins name have stamped their mark on the historical record, and one particularly colourful character was Stephen Hopkins, born in 1581 in the English county of Hampshire and one of the passengers who boarded the *Mayflower* in 1620 to escape religious persecution and establish a new life across hundreds of miles of ocean.

Details of his early life are scant, but what is known is that in June of 1609 he left his wife Mary and their young children to take up a post as a minister's clerk in Jamestown, in what was then the colony of Virginia – intending to send for his family once he had established himself.

He was aboard the *Sea Venture*, the flagship of a flotilla bound for the colony and which also carried Sir Thomas Gates, who had been appointed its new governor.

But disaster struck two months into the voyage when the ships of the flotilla were separated in a severe storm and the *Sea Venture* wrecked when forced to run aground on the shores of the island of Bermuda.

Fortunately the island had plentiful supplies of food and water that sustained the castaways as they laboured to construct enough primitive boats to take them on to their intended destination of Jamestown.

In the meantime, the autocratic Sir Thomas Gates had set himself up us 'governor' of the castaways and this rankled so much with the outspoken Hopkins that he frequently challenged his authority.

This led to him being arrested and charged with mutiny and, found guilty, sentenced to death.

Fortunately for Hopkins, however, the other castaways prevailed upon Gates to grant him a pardon.

In late May of 1610, aboard two newly constructed boats, the castaways were able to leave Bermuda behind them and at last arrive at what had been their original intended destination of Jamestown.

In addition to his clerking duties, that involved helping the minister in reading religious works to the colonists, Hopkins also appears to have worked in his original trade as a tanner.

Just as he was about to send for his family, however, word arrived from England in 1614 that his wife – who had supported herself and her children by running a tavern – had died.

Returning to England to look after his three young children and later remarrying, it was not long before the restless Hopkins set off again for the New World.

With his family in tow, this was aboard the *Mayflower,* which left Plymouth in September of 1620 bound for Virginia.

Known to posterity as the Mayflower Pilgrims or Pilgrim Fathers, Hopkins and his 102 fellow passengers were forced through severe storms to make landfall in New England – rather than Virginia – on the coast of what is now Massachusetts.

Naming their main settlement Plymouth in recognition of their departure point from England, it was here that Hopkins flourished by running a tavern until his death in 1644.

Chapter three:

Inventive genius

Bearers of the Hopkins name have also stamped their mark on the historical record through a diverse range of endeavours and pursuits that include the sciences, invention, business and academia.

Born in 1861 in Eastbourne, Sussex, Sir Frederick Hopkins was the pioneering English biochemist who in 1929 shared the Nobel Prize in Physiology or Medicine for the discovery of vitamins, having several years earlier also discovered the amino acid tryptophan.

Having studied at institutions that include the medical school at Guy's College – now part of King's College London School of Medicine – he taught physiology and toxicology for a time at the college before in 1902 joining the Physiological Laboratory at Cambridge and, twelve years later, being appointed to the chair of biochemistry at the university.

It had been in 1912 that he had published his seminal work on how diets consisting solely of fats, minerals, water, pure protein and carbohydrates are unable to support growth.

Present in normal diets, he suggested, was what

he termed "accessory food factors" – later renamed vitamins – necessary for growth and survival.

It was for his work over the following years on the nutritional value of vitamins that, along with the Dutch physiologist Christiann Eijkman, he was awarded the Nobel Prize in Physiology or Medicine.

The recipient of a host of other honours and awards that include a knighthood, the Order of Merit – Britain's most exclusive civilian honour – the Royal Medal of the scientific think-tank the Royal Society and having served for a time as president of the British Association for the Advancement of Science, he died in 1947.

From biochemistry to physics, Harold Hopkins was the British inventive genius born in the slums of Leicester in 1918.

With the encouragement of his family and teachers and through the aid of scholarships, he was able to attend a local grammar school and then University College, Leicester, graduating with a first class honours degree in physics and mathematics in 1939.

Later taking an interest in optical design, he began a research fellowship at Imperial College London in 1947, where he combined his research with teaching in the field of optics.

Taking up the chair in optics at Reading

University in 1967, it was through the application of his mathematical model known today as Hopkins Wave Theory of Aberrations that he was responsible for the invention of the zoom lens, fibre optics and rod-lens endoscopes that allow for 'key-hole' surgery.

Also having developed what is the forerunner of today's CD/DVD, nominated twice for a Nobel Prize and awarded Fellowship of the Royal Society, he died in 1994.

Pursuing a much different career path, his son Kelvin Hopkins, born in Leicester in 1941, is the British Labour Party politician who has been MP (Member of Parliament) for Luton North since 1997.

From British politics to American politics, it was in his capacity as a special adviser to President Franklin Delano Roosevelt that Harry Hopkins was one of the main architects of the president's New Deal programme of the 1930s.

A major federal relief programme to provide employment for the legions of unemployed, one aspect of the New Deal was the Works Progress Administration (WPA), which under Hopkins' direction became the largest employer in the country.

Along with Roosevelt, he was also a prime mover during the Second World War of the Lend-Lease programme to provide vital aid to beleaguered Britain.

Born in 1890 in Sioux City, Iowa and having had the onerous remit under Roosevelt of what he described as "dealing with priorities, production, political problems with allies, strategy – in short with anything that might concern the president", he died in 1946, about a year after the president he had so diligently served.

In an earlier century, Johns Hopkins was the American abolitionist and entrepreneur through whose philanthropy a number of important institutions were established.

Born in 1795 at Crofton, Maryland, one of eleven children, the family ran a plantation and were members of the Society of Friends – better known as Quakers.

In keeping with a decree from their local Quaker society in 1807, they freed the slaves who worked on their plantation giving them the choice whether to leave or continue to work for the family.

Hopkins' entrepreneurial skills first came to the fore when he was placed in temporary charge of an uncle's store when he was aged 17, and seven years later he set up his own business in partnership with fellow Quaker Benjamin Moore.

But the partnership dissolved shortly afterwards

and, along with three of his brothers, Hopkins set up Hopkins & Brothers Wholesalers.

Selling a range of wares across the Shenandoah Valley from wagons, the brothers would sometimes take corn whiskey in payment, and at great profit this was then sold in Baltimore as Hopkins' Best.

A canny investor, the bulk of Hopkins' fortune came from investment in a range of ventures that most significantly included the Baltimore and Ohio Railroad, of which he was appointed a director in 1847.

One of the wealthiest men of his time, he died in 1873, leaving bequests that led to the founding of Baltimore institutions that include the Johns Hopkins Hospital, the Johns Hopkins University – that today includes a school of medicine and a school of nursing – and the Johns Hopkins University Press.

In 1989, the U.S. Postal Service issued a stamp in his honour as part of its Great Americans series.

In contemporary times and in the realms of academia, Sir Deian Rhys Hopkins is the distinguished Welsh historian born in 1944 in Llanelli, Carmarthenshire.

A graduate in history from the University of Wales, Aberystwyth, and president of the National Library of Wales, he is a co-founder of the *Journal of Welsh People's History* while the many posts he has held include membership of the BBC General Advisory

Council and the Council for Assisting Refugee Academics (CARA).

Knighted in 2009 and the recipient of other honours that include fellowship of the Royal Historical Society, he was also appointed expert adviser to the First Minister of Wales for the centenary of the First World War.

Chapter four:

On the world stage

Bearers of the Hopkins name and its popular spelling variation of Hopkin have gained international fame and acclaim.

Born in 1937 in Margam, Port Talbot, **Anthony Hopkins**, more formally known as Sir Philip Anthony Hopkins, is the Welsh stage, television and film actor, painter and composer who is the recipient of a host of honours and awards.

The son of a baker, and influenced by the actor Richard Burton, who was also born in Port Talbot, he studied at the Royal Welsh College of Music and Drama in Cardiff, graduating from there when he was aged 20.

Training at the Royal Academy of Dramatic Art, London, after completing two years in the army during national service, his first professional stage role came in 1960 in his native Wales in a Swansea Little Theatre production of *Have a Cigarette*.

Talent-spotted by the great dramatic actor Laurence Olivier, he was invited to join the prestigious Royal National Theatre and was Olivier's understudy in a production of Strindberg's *Dance of Death* – taking over the role when the actor was struck by illness.

Despite his success on stage, Hopkins yearned for the silver screen and his first major break came in 1968 in the role of Richard I in *The Lion in Winter*.

Television roles included his portrayal of Charles Dickens in the 1970 BBC production *The Great Inimitable Mr Dickens* and that of Pierre Bezukhov in the channel's 1972 mini-series *War and Peace* – while other major film credits in the 1970s and 1980s include *A Bridge Too Far*, *The Elephant Man*, *A Change of Seasons* and *Bounty*.

Starring opposite Emma Thompson in the 1993 *The Remains of the Day*, he was nominated for an Academy Award for Best Actor, while receiving the BAFTA Award for Best Actor in the same year for *Shadowlands*, based on the life of C.S. Lewis.

His best known role, however, is his chilling portrayal of the cannibalistic serial killer Dr Hannibal Lecter in the 1991 *The Silence of the Lambs* – for which he won an Academy Award for Best Actor – the 2001 *Hannibal* and, from 2002, *Red Dragon*.

With other screen credits that include the 2005 *The World's Fastest Indian* and the 2011 *The Rite* and narrator of the 2000 Dr Seuss' *How the Grinch Stole Christmas*, he is the recipient of a star on the Hollywood Walk of Fame and both a CBE and a knighthood for services to the arts.

Also the recipient of the Golden Globe Cecil B. DeMille Award for Lifetime Achievement and the BAFTA Academy Fellowship Award, the actor is known for his support of a number of charities and appeals.

As president of the National Trust's Snowdonia Appeal, he has helped to raise funds for the Snowdonia National Park in the north of Wales – donating £1m of his own money to the appeal in 1998.

A wing of the Royal Welsh College of Music and Drama has been named the Anthony Hopkins Centre in his honour.

Known for his role of Sergeant Dan Scott in fourteen episodes of the television series *Midsomer Murders*, **John Hopkins** is the actor of stage, television and film born in London in 1974.

Winner of the Best Actor Award at the *Sunday Times* National Student Drama Festival while he was a member from 1993 to 1996 of the Leeds University Union Theatre Group for his role of Nathan in *A Short Play about Sex and Death*, other television credits include *Secret Diary of a Call Girl* and the American mini-series *The Path to 9/11*.

Other stage credits include, for the Royal Shakespeare Company, *The Tempest* and *Antony and Cleopatra*, while big screen credits include the 2010 *Alice in Wonderland*.

Behind the camera lens, John Richard Hopkins, credited as **John R. Hopkins**, was the English stage, television and film writer born in London in 1931.

A writer during the 1960s for the popular BBC police drama series *Z-Cars* in addition to the four-part play *Talking to a Stranger* and his adaptation of John le Carré's *Smiley's People*, he died in 1998.

One of the most renowned set and production designers of his time, **George Hopkins** was born in 1896 in Pasadena, California.

Winner of five Academy Awards – for the 1943 *Mission to Moscow*, the 1951 *A Streetcar Named Desire*, the 1964 *My Fair Lady*, the 1966 *Who's Afraid of Virginia Woolf?* and the 1969 *Hello Dolly!* he died in 1985.

In the world of contemporary media celebrity, **Katie Hopkins** is the British television personality and journalist born in 1975 in Barnstaple, Devon.

The daughter of an electrical engineer, it was in 2007 that she first came to fame as a contestant on the reality television programme *The Apprentice*.

Having subsequently appeared on other television reality shows that include *Celebrity Big Brother* and *I'm a Celebrity ...Get Me Out of Here!* she is also a controversial columnist for a British tabloid newspaper.

Bearers of the Hopkins name have excelled in the highly competitive world of sport.

In the boxing ring, **Bernard Hopkins, Jr.**, born in Philadelphia in 1965, is the American champion who, having fought as both a light heavyweight and as a middleweight is ranked by *The Ring* boxing magazine at No.3 in its list of the ten best middleweight title holders.

From the boxing ring to the cricket pitch, **John Hopkins**, born in 1953 in Maesteg, Mid Glamorgan is the Welsh former part time wicket keeper and right-handed batsman who played for more than seventeen years with Glamorgan.

Also a right-handed batsman and also having fielded as a wicket keeper for Glamorgan, **Jeffris Hopkins** was born in 1950 in Bridgend, Glamorgan; also having played for Middlesex, he was part of the Welsh team in the 1979 ITC Trophy competition.

On the fields of European football and in the early Hopkins heartland of Wales, **Jeff Hopkins**, born in 1964 in Swansea, is the former international defender who played for teams that include Reading, Fulham and Crystal Palace and coached teams that include Australia's Brisbane Roar women's team.

From sport to music, Gaynor Hopkins is the best-selling Welsh singer better known by her stage name of **Bonnie Tyler**.

Born in 1951 in Skewen, near Neath, Port Talbot, the daughter of a coal miner, she was aged seventeen when one of her aunts entered her into a talent contest.

Finishing in second place after giving her renditions of the Ray Charles song *I Can't Stop Loving You* and fellow Welsh songstress Mary Hopkin's hit *Those Were The Days*, she has gone on to enjoy a string of top-selling singles and albums.

These include *It's a Heartache*, *Holding Out for a Hero*, *Total Eclipse of the Heart*, *Bitterblue* and *Believe in Me*, while in 2013, two years after being made a freeman of her native Neath for her lifelong contribution in the field of entertainment, she was presented with a British Academy of Songwriters, Composers and Authors' (BASCA) Award.

The Welsh singer from whom she took inspiration in the formative stages of her career was **Mary Hopkin**, born in 1950 in Pontardawe, Swansea.

One of the first artists to be signed to the Beatles' Apple recording label, she is best known for her 1968 hit international single *Those Were The Days*.

Placed second in the 1970 Eurovision Song Contest, representing the United Kingdom, with *Knock Knock, Who's There?* she is also now known by her married name of Mary Visconti.

In a totally different musical genre, **John Henry Hopkins, Jr.,** was the American Episcopalian clergyman and hymnist best known for his 1863 composition *We Three Kings of Orient Are*.

Born in 1820 in Pittsburgh and having delivered the eulogy in 1885 at the funeral of President Ulysses S. Grant, he died in 1891.

From the creative world of music to the equally creative world of the written word, **John Hopkins**, born in 1938 in Orange, New Jersey, is the American writer whose acclaimed works include his 1972 *Tangier Buzzless Flies* and the 1983 *The Flight of the Pelican*.

Shortlisted in 2010 for the book industry's Queen of Teen Award, **Cathy Hopkins** is the English novelist born in 1953 in Manchester.

Known for her *Mates, Dates* series, she has also collaborated with the cartoonist Gray Jolliffe.

From prose to poetry, **Gerard Manley Hopkins** was the Victorian poet and Jesuit priest more formally known as the Reverend Father Gerard Manley Hopkins.

Born in 1844 in Stratford, Essex, one of nine children and whose father had at one time been British consul general in Hawaii, it was while studying classics at Oxford that he composed his acclaimed 1866 poem *The Habit of Perfection*, while in the same year he converted to the Roman Catholic faith.

Becoming a Jesuit priest, he resolved to dedicate his life to religion – to the extent that for another seven years he almost entirely gave up writing poetry.

But the creative urge proved too strong and Hopkins went on to pen other noted works that include his 1875 *The Wreck of the Deutschland* – a poem inspired by the sinking of the vessel of the name and the death of 157 people who had included five Franciscan nuns who had been fleeing Germany because of what were then its harsh anti-Catholic laws.

Curate for a time at St Aloysius's Church, Oxford and also having ministered in Manchester and Glasgow, he died in 1889.

A leading figure in the late 1960s in the music and fashion scene known as "Swinging London", John Hopkins, better known as **Hoppy Hopkins**, was the English photographer, journalist and political activist born in 1937.

Turning his back on a planned career as a nuclear physicist in favour of photo-journalism after graduating when he was aged 20 from Cambridge University, he went on to capture the images of many of the most famous figures of his generation.

These included the Beatles and the Rolling Stones, while he also took iconic images of 'countercultural' figures including the American poet Allen Ginsberg and the American black activist Malcolm X.

Arrested in 1967 for possession of cannabis, he became the centre of media attention when sentenced to nine months in prison – with the judge sternly describing him as "a pest to society".

Released after six months, with a number of leading celebrities having supported the "Free Hoppy" campaign, Hopkins, who died in 2015, had also been instrumental along with others in setting up the London Free School in Notting Hill – forerunner of the annual multi-cultural celebration The Notting Hill Carnival.